William Faulkner: A Life on Paper

William Faulkner
A Life On Paper

A TRANSCRIPTION FROM THE FILM
PRODUCED BY
THE MISSISSIPPI CENTER
FOR EDUCATIONAL TELEVISION

FUNDING PROVIDED IN PART BY
A GRANT FROM THE
NATIONAL ENDOWMENT FOR
THE HUMANITIES

Script by A. I. Bezzerides

Introduction by Carvel Collins

Adapted and Edited by Ann Abadie

Published by the
University Press of Mississippi
in cooperation with the
Mississippi Authority for Educational Television
Jackson
1980

"William Faulkner: A Life on Paper" was broadcast
nationally on the Public Broadcasting Service on
December 17, 1979. The film was rebroadcast on
August 11, 1980.

Library of Congress Cataloging in Publication Data

Bezzerides, Albert Isaac, 1908–
    William Faulkner, a life on paper.

    1. Faulkner, William, 1897–1962. 2. Authors,
American—20th century—Biography. I. Title
PS3511.A86Z6283   813'.5'2 [B]   79-15371
ISBN 0-87805-098-1

Contents

Preface

by A. I. Bezzerides

Years ago, more years ago than I dare admit, I saw a slightly
built man, with graying hair, a mustache, his hand around
the bowl of a pipe, the stem jutted into his mouth, sitting
in a back-booth in the Pig-'n-Whistle restaurant on Hollywood Boulevard, in Hollywood, California. Although I had
never seen him before, beyond a portrait on a jacket or a
photograph accompanying a review, I experienced instant
recognition. It was hardly what one would describe as
casual recognition, in which one murmurs a name, but one
that was inwardly howled. Ordinary print can hardly do
justice to the howl. The letters would have to be capi-
talized, printed in fire, the exclamations slashed with a
razor—MY GOD, IT'S WILLIAM FAULKNER!

Some years before that, Yvonne von Gorne, my girl-
friend, later my wife, had given me a copy of *As I Lay Dying*
for my birthday, the reading of which became an experience I have not forgotten to this day. I was then an engineering student at the University of California at Berkeley
and had read widely from the day I could read, every book
I could lay my hands on, that William Saroyan had not
beaten me to, in the Fresno, California, Library. I remember vividly my reactions as I dug into Faulkner's novel.

At first I was puzzled, then alarmed, then confused by
the layers of meaning that lay beneath meanings that lay
beneath the juxtaposition of simple words. Alarmed,
doubting my sanity, baffled, frustrated, angered, I read on
into the book, turning back as many if not more pages than
I read, in a futile effort to make sense out of seeming nonsense. Yet I knew, somehow, that every word, everything
I read, had to make sense. Even so, I stopped now and
then, frothing at the mouth, to fling the book across the

6

room against the wall, until finally the book flew apart, scattered pages in every direction.

I cursed the day the book had been given to me, pondered what malicious intent my girl-friend must have had to give me such a perverse gift, vowed never again, ever, to read it or anything else Faulkner wrote. After which, I found myself picking up the violated book, reassembling its scrambled pages, absolutely compelled to read on, only to find myself slipping into still another fit of temper. This happened again and again until somehow I had finished the book or the book had finished me, to this day I can't decide which.

Indeed, I read it again and again. And after that, certain that I had entirely lost my mind, I read everything that Faulkner wrote. As the books were published and the stories appeared, I read with the same inexplicable, confounding, passionate fascination and again experienced the self-doubt, frustration, and rage.

In order to write the script on William Faulkner, I read all the books and stories over again, and found myself making discoveries anew, as if I had not read them properly the first time. I experienced an entirely new experience, this time not from the perspective of a young man in his twenties, but that of an old crock in his sixties. His writing now provokes in me an entirely new evaluation of him as a writer—that his work, which is said to relate not only to the South, but to the whole world, relates to the reader not in some singular unique way, but in a variety of complex ways that change as the reader himself grows older and changes.

So now, *there he was*, William Faulkner himself, in the Pig-'n-Whistle, of all places, sitting in a booth, sipping tea! I found myself struggling to my feet, stumbling past waiters and patrons, barging my way to the booth where he sat with a woman companion. I lunged in to interrupt their tete-a-tete, announcing (in a voice that I could not control, hearing myself shout and wondering all the while why on earth I was shouting) that though he could not possibly

7

know me from Adam, I certainly knew him, who he was, that I had read everything he had written, that though I understood little of what he wrote, I thought he was a great writer, that I hoped one day to mature to his work, possibly even to the point of understanding it. Chuckling, Faulkner rose to his feet, pipe in hand, responded to my bellowed praise in an astonishingly meek voice; "Thank you, suh. . . ." Whereupon I spun around and staggered back to my friends in the booth.

Some years after that, I had abandoned the security of engineering for the insecurity of writing. The year was 1944. I was sitting in my office at Warner Brothers' Studios, in Burbank, California, when who should I see, pipe-bowl in fist, stem in mouth, pass through the secretarial ward and enter the office next to mine, where he dropped into an easychair, crossed his legs, and sat puffing his pipe. Despite the air of frigid inviolability, of preferred isolation that Faulkner always radiated, I entered his office, and stood before him. This time, I am pleased to remember, I was not so stunned or so worshipful or so hysterical, and my voice was more controlled. I asked if he remembered me.

I remember the swift upcast look the quick nod, the odd wry smile, as he removed the pipe-stem from his mouth, "Anh-hanh, I certainly do." This was during World War II, when transportation was hard to come by. I offered him a ride into Hollywood, he accepted, and later that afternoon I drove him to the Highland Hotel, where he lived. After that I picked him up every work-day morning and dropped him off every afternoon, and that is how we became friends.

At one point in our friendship, before circumstances parted us—he to return defiantly to Oxford, Mississippi, to sit out the indenture of his Warner Brothers' contract, and I to go on to Paramount Studios—Faulkner made a remark that seemed strange to me at the time. "Bud," he said, "someday you'll be writing about me."

I knew how private he was, how infuriated he became when his privacy was intruded upon, so I hastened to assure him that I would never write about him. Yet, despite my assurance that I would not write about him, it turns out that I have.

I find myself wondering how this came about. It's a long story and I do not intend to go into it here, but the fact is that I did write about him. I wrote about him for more than two years. I edited the same script again and again to satisfy the demands of a snarl of professors who had their own ideas about how my script should be written. I wrote and wrote, when I had vowed, not only to Faulkner but to myself as well, that I would not leap to write about him as had so many others, each with his own story to tell, inventing a new Faulkner in the process.

I had read so many things about Faulkner, one of which was a script that missed the man altogether. It seemed to me that I could explore Faulkner's past, assemble facts, capture some aspect of the Faulkner that had escaped the others. I had myself been struggling for a long time now, trying to become the writer I had hoped to be. I knew that something more than the simple desire to become a writer was necessary, something more than going to classes, study-ing under professors, who thought they could teach the mystique of writing, even though only a few could write themselves. I hoped, by touching on Faulkner's life, to gain some clue, however accidentally, as to how he had come to write the things he had written. For all my good inten-tions, during the process of researching and writing the script, I discovered how difficult it is to say all there is to say about a person, especially if that person is famous. All his friends, his relatives, his acquaintances, his admirers, and especially the professors, who teach Faulkner I-A and I-B in the universities, and who deleted everything they thought to be offensive, because they respected Faulkner's image more than they did the all too fallible man, distorted reality not so much by controlling what was said as by con-trolling what was not said. The logic was used that Faulkner believed that a man's work should be allowed to speak for him, that a man's private life was inviolable. Yet I knew that

9

his privacy was bound to be violated, as it was in the lengthy biography that was published. I knew Faulkner well enough to know that if his privacy was to be violated, he would want it to be told as it was, warts and all. Faulkner would have balked at being corrupted into legend, out of misguided deference to some concocted image, at cost to the man. Certainly, it would have seemed ridiculous to him that a man could live a life, only to have the most vital aspects of the life he had lived, the life that had made him the man he was, edited and censored out from under him.

But no matter. When I first read Faulkner, there were few who understood or could explain him. But the young reader today has available to him a whole body of work to guide him through the labyrinthine complexes of his work. And here now is still another book which contains interviews with people who knew Faulkner. But they are bound to be reserved and discreet, just as I was bound to be reserved and discreet, all of us too awed by the image to pay due homage to the man himself.

Introduction

by Carvel Collins

In 1974, after initial urging by George Wolfe of the University of Alabama, the Mississippi Authority for Educational Television asked the National Endowment for the Humanities to grant financial aid to make a film about William Faulkner. When the National Endowment handsomely responded, Mississippi ETV selected as producer a widely experienced member of its staff, Walt Lowe.

He hired A. I. Bezzerides as script writer and enlisted consultations from several critics and professors of American literature. In 1976, after Bezzerides had written the script, Lowe hired me to help with the film in any way I could; so the random personal impressions and recollections about the making of the film which I have been asked to jot down for this book can only begin at that point.

The first impression was that making a documentary about Faulkner was an excellent project, for many serious critics worldwide have come to consider him the best novelist the United States has produced so far in this century. And it seemed that the sooner the film could be made, the better, for the number of people who had known Faulkner well and could be photographed was steadily shrinking, as I was aware from personal experience because more than half of the few hundred people I had interviewed about him since 1947 had died.

The next reaction, though, was an anxious one—that to accomplish the compression necessary for a two-hour film about the life and works of a complex genius who wrote more than a score of books and lived more than sixty years would be difficult at best. Documentary films on painters, sculptors, and dramatists have plenty to present which is visual, essential to the subject, and sometimes rather quickly perceived, even when only superficially. But what is important about a good novelist is, of course, the novels, and they make enormous difficulties for film: they cannot be read aloud into the microphone in their entirety, and snippets quoted from them cannot show the overall movement and total structure that are among the glories of good fiction. To dramatize a few scenes is not always effective, for they too are just snippets and, besides, if Faulkner, say, had wanted *Light in August* to appear as a play, he would not have written it as a novel, a remarkably different thing. Even documentary films about the politically prominent can show them accepting nominations or pausing with their spouses beside ballot boxes, but two hours filmed of a novelist pecking at a typewriter are bound to pall.

Another early and worrisome impression was that the divisions which exist in the professional critical interpretation of Faulkner's works might make the preparation of the film difficult. One of the factions, the largest and the longest established, holds that a chief or even the chief value of novels by Faulkner is their historical and sociological depiction of life in his region of the United States. One part of this view which was expressed early and became widely accepted holds that Faulkner was not able to organize each of his works adequately, that they therefore fail aesthetically, but that they are nevertheless important because when strung together as a series they give the reader knowledge about the long history of a region's life. An opposite faction in professional interpretation of Faulkner believes that most of his novels are to be viewed not primarily as parts of a somewhat journalistic series but as individual artistic objects and that, far from being disorganized, they are skillfully structured aesthetically to make their effects—effects which are not primarily historical or sociological. Faulkner showed some agreement with this critical view when he said in 1956, "... it does sort of amuse me when I hear 'em talking about the sociological picture that I present in something like *As I Lay Dying*, for instance."

A useful illustration of the opposition of these two extremes among the critical factions is to note with much oversimplification the differences between some of their interpretations of a sample Faulkner novel, *Absalom, Absalom!* The faction oriented toward social science considers that the character Thomas Sutpen is the novel's most significant element and that the account of his making a plantation out of wilderness is a—or the—main value in the novel. This reductive conception of the purpose of *Absalom, Absalom!* understandably leads to doubt about Faulkner's abilities as an artist, for surely the best way to present the story of Sutpen as the developer of a plantation would simply be to tell it in chronological order, but the form which Faulkner gave to *Absalom, Absalom!* is far from chronological, and several of the major aspects of Sutpen's life are shown to be merely invented by two other characters, Quentin Compson and a fellow student at Harvard. Many readers, therefore, find the form of that novel artistically defective because it is not efficiently shaped to present what some critics have told them the novel is trying to say. The extreme opposite faction of professional critics considers that in *Absalom, Absalom!* one of the primary concerns is psychological, with Quentin Compson as a central figure, and that the novel's involute structure is an aesthetically efficient and successful form for presenting Quentin's complicated emotional and mental condition. Readers who accept this later view often decide that Faulkner, after all, knew what he was trying to do and that he proved his high rank as an artist by knowing how to do it.

The makers of the film—Lowe, Bezzerides, and the director, Robert Squier—have dealt imaginatively with those and other difficulties inherent in their subject and have made a film that seems to have been well received at a trial showing in Mississippi before its scheduled national appearance on the public broadcasting network later this year. Though I have not seen the very final cut of the film

13

or read the final form of the script printed here, the next-to-final versions of both showed that, concerning the split among critics of Faulkner's works, the makers of the film, accepting most of the argument, have done much to avoid producing a film which would bear the same relationship to those critical views of Faulkner which seem likely to predominate in the future that the last buggy whip factory bore to Henry Ford's assembly line. And they have dealt with the problem of the vast amount of extant information about William Faulkner and his writings by giving much of the film's footage to excerpts from interviews with people who had known Faulkner, most of them his family, friends, or professional associates. With great energy the staff arranged an admirably large number of interviews, in Mississippi, Virginia, California, Louisiana, New York, Alabama, Connecticut, and France. The people being interviewed were invariably generous with their time and memories, and good humored in the extreme as camera crews invaded their homes from the Ile Saint-Louis to Santa Monica. The greatest single asset of the film is the interview with William Faulkner's daughter, Mrs. Jill Faulkner Summers, in which she movingly combines objectivity and affection. In her interview and many of the others the only disappointment is that by the nature of things the film's time limits forced the exclusion of so much of what was said.

Another of the attractive features of the film is the large number of old photographs that the staff was able to borrow and let the camera rove over during the narration by Raymond Burr and the quoting from Faulkner's writing done in an approximation of Faulkner's voice by Arthur Ed Forman.

Walt Lowe has been director and producer of successful films, one of them an outstanding study of D. W. Griffith. Buzz Bezzerides is widely known and experienced as a skilled and successful screen writer and novelist, and in addition knew William Faulkner well in Hollywood. Bob Squier has made successful films of several kinds, some of them early for one of the leaders among educational television stations, WGBH of Boston, and is now making more for his own active organization, The Communications Company in Washington, D.C.

Considering the cliché jokes about the weakness of decisions by committees, it was surprising, and certainly pleasant, to find that these makers of the film were able to disprove the clichés by their effective operation of the committee action on which constructing a documentary film of this sort inevitably depends. For such skilled professionals to bring their artistic and technical experience to this documentary out of a genuine interest in its subject, and often at financial loss to themselves, meant that argument about the content and tenor of the film was always intense and seriously reasoned. But their sophistication and wit made it always amiable. Because of that amiability, humor turned out to be the most effective rhetorical weapon in the inevitable battle between the desire for an interesting film and the desire for an accurate one. Usually, because of the good nature of the continual discussions, it became apparent quickly enough that those two desires were not inherently in conflict.

One among the many pleasant recollections of the working sessions during the planning is of hearing Shelby Foote give to several of the discussions the benefit of his years of friendship with William Faulkner, his great knowledge of Southern history, and his perceptions as a gifted novelist.

When the planning resolved into shooting the film, it was good also to spend time again with so many people who had been open-handed with information about Faulkner years before. Abnormal and often quite saddening awareness of the passage of time, that all things change, is a problem for anyone trying to study the recent past. To study the life and times of Dante or Sophocles probably is not so saddening; they are far enough away to be safely in History. But continually to read newspapers and letters written only a few decades ago and to be continually asking survivors of the recent past to recall their youth can begin to pile up an effect until at the end of a working day one turns for relief to that evening's newspaper and the illogical but comforting illusion that Now is real and lasting. So it was with considerable hesitation that I accepted the invitation to accompany Walt Lowe and Bob Squier to France to film interviews with a number of people I had questioned concerning Faulkner about fifteen years before, hesitation because seeing them again might lay one more level on the sobering effect of observing first-hand the changes time can bring. But the trip was a most pleasant surprise. All of those filmed seemed unharmed by the passage of recent years and, as Walt and Bob elicited the best from them, were as intelligently informative and entertaining as they had ever been. Mrs. William Aspenwall Bradley, who had placed some of Faulkner's works for European publication and whose late husband had contributed fundamentally in 1918 to the concepts and materials Faulkner used more than thirty-five years later in A Fable, was, in her eighties, as perceptive and distinguished as she always had been in judging thought and character. V. P. Ferguson, who as a student at Ole Miss had known Faulkner and has been for several years a successful writer in France, was just as effectively and effervescently witty and as penetrating as ever. And all the others interviewed on film in France seemed to have set time aside. The same, I may say, seemed true of most of the people interviewed on film in Oxford, where the physical surroundings of Faulkner's life, the town and the University, while keeping intact much of what Faulkner lived with, almost seem to have changed more than the people who knew him well and who consistently gave for this film excellent interviews in which they appeared to be only lightly touched, if at all, by the time which had run by since they first let me talk with them about Oxford's most distinguished citizen.

After years of wandering here and there trying to learn about William Faulkner, armed only with pad, pencil, small recorder, and a still camera, it was good to be present while skilled technicians under solid financing worked with excellent equipment, including a Steadicam and an out-board camera mount for helicopters—which brings up a recollection of the personal sort that has been asked for here, even though it is mostly a selfish one.

Faulkner's great-grandfather, W. C. Falkner, known as the Old Colonel, is buried in the cemetery at Ripley, Mississippi, where at the top of a tall stone column stands his statue, dominating the cemetery and gazing toward the modernized tracks of the railroad he built nearly a century ago. Many photographs of the statue have been taken by cameras aimed upward from the ground, but for years, beginning in 1948, I had tried by various means to make an exposure from some base elevated to the statue's level. And always I had failed. Then, during one of the 1977 sessions of filming in Mississippi, Walt Lowe leased a mobile camera crane from Atlanta for some work in Oxford. To my delight, when Bob Squier took one of the crews to Ripley, the crane went along. It was extremely useful for, among other shots, smoothly letting the camera pan didactically and dramatically across the cemetery from the monument bearing the family name of the man who killed Faulkner's great-grandfather to the name at the base of the monument of his victim and then rise to its top. So it was a selfish pleasure, after so many years, to see, because of the good equipment, that up in the air on a level with the statue was at last a camera. There was even an additional selfish gain: when the crew finished and was packing up for the run back to Oxford, Bob, ever generous, let me use the crane with a still camera. So, twenty-nine years after the first of several bungled attempts—two dented car roofs, one collapsed triangular stack of long ladders, several insufficiently stable camera poles, and a flimsy wooden structure blown away by the wind—it was inordinately satisfying to be looking at last through a finder, eyeball to stone eyeball with the lightly lichen-flecked Old Colonel.

In 1978, in the spring, Walt Lowe phoned from Jackson, Mississippi, to say that the material selected for inclusion in the film timed out to about four hours but the finished film was to run for less than two. He asked me to come to Jackson to help him cut the material in half. At the dining table in his apartment we settled down to steady work interrupted only by occasional brief breaks of restorative observation from the dining room window beneath which lay a swimming pool of the singles apartment complex. Charming as were the local endowments, turning from the window back to the work financed by the National one was easy because the drastic cutting was solving several problems. The amount of documentably false "information" about William Faulkner's life and writing that has been solidly established in print over the decades and firmly believed to be true is surely greater than that for any other modern writer. Cooperative and amiable as the many planning sessions for shooting the film has been, some generally believed misconceptions were inevitably persistent because of the size and firm establishment of that body of non-fact. Now, with the necessity to reduce the length of the film by half, it was easy to move some of even the most persistent confusions into the discard.

More recently, when Bob Squier asked me to come to Washington to give reactions as his staff projected the next-to-final cut of the film in his offices at The Communications Company, he was as willing as he and his colleagues had always been to make revisions after listening to arguments against the remaining documentable inaccuracies of occasional passages in the statements selected from the filmed interviews or of the sequences in which items were presented or of the relationships implied by the way the camera moved over old photographs and drawings. So that final session wound up with only a few disagreements unresolved.

The makers of the film, faced with remarkable difficulties, seem to have brought off a satisfactory result. And responses to the film's trial presentation on Mississippi Educational Television last May support that opinion. Ben Wasson, who should be a good judge, for he is not only perceptive but knew William Faulkner extremely well in

Mississippi, New York, and California from 1919 until Faulkner's death in 1962, phoned immediately after its Mississippi showing to express his delight in the film. And his review the next day in his regular arts column for the Greenville, Mississippi, *Delta-Democrat* must have pleased Walt Lowe and Buzz Bezzerides and Bob Squier because it calls their film "a truly splendid achievement."

The first time we met Walt said he had the paradoxical hope that after the film appeared nationally on the public broadcasting network a number of its viewers would switch off their television sets and read a Faulkner novel. That hope of his may very well become a reality.

Vista, California

Editor's Note

Only the narrator and the speakers are identified in the script. For distinction, the passages read in "Faulkner's Voice" are set in italic, with the source of the quoted material added in parentheses.

No captions are used with the photographs because their placement indicates the person or scene referred to in the script. It is not possible to capture in printed form the full visual effect of the film. However, many of the still photographs and selected frames from the film are reproduced here. Because the documentary film was prepared for television, the stills and the frame enlargements are reproduced in the format of a TV screen.

Ann Abadie
Oxford, Mississippi

William Faulkner
A Life On Paper

... the entire valley stretched beneath him ... wrapped in peace
and quiet beneath the evening sun, as it had slept for a century;
waiting invisibly honey-combed with joys and sorrows, hopes and
despairs, for the end of time. . . . For a while he stood on one
horizon and stared across at the other far above a world of
endless toil and troubled slumber; untouched, untouchable, and
as the sun released him who lived and labored in the sun, his
mind that troubled him for the first time became quieted. ("The
Hill")

*... the old verities and truths of the heart, the old universal
truths lacking which any story is ephemeral and doomed—love
and honor and pity and pride and compassion and sacrifice ...*

*... the poet's, the writer's duty is to write about these things.
It is his privilege to help man endure by lifting his heart, by
reminding him of the courage and honor and hope and pride
and compassion and pity and sacrifice which have been the glory
of his past.* (Nobel Prize Acceptance Speech)

Shelby Foote.   His talent lies in something that's easily
stated and is very hard to do and that is his ability to com-
municate sensation, tell you what something feels like or
what goes on inside you when you see certain things.

*The poets are wrong of course ... but then, poets are almost
always wrong about the facts. That's because they are not interested in facts: only in truth, which is why the truth they speak
is so true that even those who hate poets by simple natural
instinct are exalted and terrified by it.*

Narrator.   This is Lafayette County, Mississippi, but when William Faulkner wrote about it he called it Yoknapatawpha County. All the land. All the people on the land.

William Faulkner, sole owner and proprietor of Yoknapatawpha County, somewhere in the state of Mississippi.

In the beginning it was virgin—to the west, along the Big River, the alluvial swamps threaded by black almost motionless bayous

and impenetrable with cane and buckvine and cypress and ash and oak and gum; to the east, the hardwood ridges and the prairies where the Appalachian Mountains died and buffalo grazed; to the south, the pine barrens and the moss-hung live-oaks and the greater swamps less of earth than water . . . where Louisiana in its time would begin. ("Mississippi")

Narrator.   This is Oxford, Mississippi, in Lafayette County, as it is today . . . a small town as towns go and strictly speaking not Faulkner's mythical town of Jefferson in Yoknapatawpha County. But aspects of the town he created can be found here, reminders of how it was, what he made of it when he lived here and wrote the books.

It was from this town, from this countryside, from these

23

people that Faulkner drew the materials which shaped the poems, the stories, and the novels that comprise his body of work. It was this South that nourished his need to write. To make, as he said, his scratch on the face of anonymity.

Frenchman's Bend was a section of rich river-bottom country lying twenty miles southeast of Jefferson. Hill-cradled and remote, definite yet without boundaries, straddling into two counties and owing allegiance to neither, it had been the original grant and site of a tremendous pre–Civil War plantation, the ruins of which—the gutted shell of an enormous house with its fallen stables and slave quarters and overgrown gardens were still known as the Old Frenchman's place. (The Hamlet)

Narrator. How did the people of Oxford, his family, his friends, his neighbors, see William Faulkner when he was no more than a would-be writer in their midst?

Phil Mullen. To them he was just little Billy Faulkner. He was broke most of the time; he owed bills all over town all the time so he just wasn't very popular in Oxford.

M. R. Hall. Yea, he's 'culia. He'd come and me and him would sit on a bench, and we would talk. D'reckly he'd git up and go. I'd wonder about it. And so he'd come back, and I'd say, "Mr. Faulkner, you kinda slipped off and left me." He said, "Yeah, when I think of something, I've got to go."

And that was it. I'd maybe be shoeing his horse and it all would be the same way.

Wade Ward. He had a man down there topping some trees for 'em, Will McGee, and he climbed up in the tree and cut a rotten limb out of it. And there was a snake in that hole—right at the limb hole, and he jumped plum out of the tree—liked to have killed hisself. That's right, and he go to get a stick to kill the snake, and Mr. William

27

wouldn't let him kill 'em. And, he wouldn't let him kill a snake, and he'd go out and check his birds and he would feed the birds. He'd put feed out on the lawn for the birds. He didn't want to kill nothing, not even insects.

Thomas Clark.   Oxford is built around a town square with the courthouse in the middle with those two drug stores, the Rolle drug store and the Gathright-Reed drug store. Well, students went into those places all the time and they were favorite places with William Faulkner.

Motee Daniels. And I've seen him stand there in front of Blaylock's drug store and look over that statue there and look like he was froze there.

Mac Reed. He was wondering if somebody tied in with one of his characters. I think that he certainly did want to have the privilege of seeing people that he might know.

Taylor McElroy.   You might see him riding a horse some day, all liveried up as they say—had on the dress like a colonel. Then he'd come out here with long whiskers and look like a hippie.

Motee Daniels.   I just really don't think anybody really knew what kinda fella William Faulkner was. He was so moody. He just soon go downtown with a pair of house shoes on or a pair of pajamas or something—he didn't care.

Narrator. This was how the town saw Faulkner for much of his life. They thought of him as a drunk. Although he could, if he chose, go for months on end without drinking at all.

Jill Faulkner Summers. He used drinking as a safety valve. It had to come out some way and almost invariably at the end of a book. First few days, as I said, Pappy would be extremely active. He'd want to do things. And then, one morning he would be a little quieter than he had been and all of a sudden he would start on his poem that heralded one of these bouts coming on: "when daisies pied and violets blue and ladies smocks all silver white, and cowslip bells with yellow hue that paint the meadow with light." On and on and on. And you knew that the next day he'd be drinking. That was just the beginning of it.

Narrator. For too long a time they saw him as a failure having neither goals nor ambitions, squandering his life, scribbling.

George Plimpton. He used to say the best place a writer could find to work was a bordello because it was

quieter there in the morning and you weren't interrupted, and in the evening it had a social life if you wanted that; and the girls all called you "Sir," so did the madam and the police, and all you needed was a cigarette and a little bourbon and paper and a pencil—that was all you needed.

Narrator. Even when the books began to come out, one after another, people were unaware of what was happening.

Emily Whitehurst Stone. Bill's uncle, Judge Falkner, was so outdone with Bill, he said, "Hell, he ain't ever going to amount to a damn—not a damn."

Shelby Foote.   If you came to Oxford in the late '30s, say, and down on the Square you asked someone where William Faulkner lived, he would be apt to turn his head and spit. The town resented *Sanctuary*, for instance, when Faulkner was known as a corn-cob man, and they thought he was sullying the atmosphere.

Robert Penn Warren.   They simply did not understand

the world he was writing about. They just simply could not grasp it. Over and over again you'd hear that. Even reviewers couldn't grasp it. And they couldn't grasp, somehow, the non-local importance of Faulkner.

Narrator.   In 1897, in this house in New Albany, Mississippi, William Faulkner was born to Maud Butler and Murry Falkner. He was the first of four Falkner boys. His father,

Murry, settled down to work for his father, J. W. T. Falkner, called the "Young Colonel," who owned the controlling interest in the Gulf and Chicago Line, all sixty miles of it. It had been built by his father, the "Old Colonel," a self-made lawyer, soldier, planter, and writer of vast persistence and energy. In his prime he had written *The White Rose of Memphis*, which remained the best-selling novel for decades. Given to violence, he was twice acquitted of murder, and was eventually murdered himself by a business rival.

So there were railroads in the land now . . . so that the rich
Northerners could come down in comfort and open the land
indeed: setting up with their Yankee dollars the vast lumbering
plants and mills in the southern pine section, the little towns

which had been hamlets without change or alteration for fifty years, booming and soaring into cities overnight. ("Mississippi")

Narrator.   William's father, Murry, worked as a passenger agent for the Gulf and Chicago Line and dreamed of one day inheriting his father's share of the railroad. But in June, 1902, the Young Colonel exercised his controlling interest and sold the family railroad.

On September 22, 1902, William's father, Murry, moved his family to Oxford, Mississippi.

In those days children started schooling when their parents chose. Maud did not enroll her children until they were eight, so the Faulkner boys had the whole long days to play.

Murry Falkner.   We played baseball and flew kites. We all had ponies. Our father was a great horseman. I remember, he had us riding ponies as soon as we were able to sit on top of them. And we read a lot.

Our mother loved literature and could become completely immersed in it. The world really didn't exist when she was reading something. Our father would confine himself generally to cowboy stories.

Narrator.   As a child Faulkner could be fun-loving, outgoing, when he chose. But by the time his youngest brother, Dean, was born in 1907, William was beginning to withdraw, become private, be given to long brooding silences like his mother. And as he grew older, he began to think of becoming a writer like his great-grandfather, the Old Colonel. His father and grandfather conspired to make him work in the old man's bank. Faulkner hated it, protested, for he thought working for money was a contemptible thing.

And then when Faulkner was 18, Estelle Oldham, his child-hood playmate, went away to finishing school in Staunton,

Virginia. Years earlier she had vowed to marry him. William missed her terribly. He wrote her long letters, sent her drawings and, using Swinburne and Housman as models, wrote her the poetry of youth. Phil Stone, a friend of the family, had read the early poetry, and decided Faulkner had talent.

Emily Whitehurst Stone.   Phil went up to Yale and found out about the imagists and the symbolists and all this new stuff that was breaking through in the world of literature, and he was just on fire with it. And here was Bill down here in a little country town, and there was nobody there who was interested in this sort of thing. So they got

to know one another and they would go walking for miles out on a place east of Oxford called Woodson Ridge, beautiful in the spring with pines and dogwood, and they would walk 12 or 14 or 16 miles a day, with Phil talking about literature and Bill listening.

Narrator.   Stone once wrote, "Faulkner had an aristocratic, superior appearance, which most people considered an affectation, an aloof reserve and an arrogant snappishness when someone tried to get familiar."

Ben Wasson.   He admired everything that was British and dressed in what he thought was a British manner and had a rather grand air on the campus. The students at that time called him "Count No Count."

Emily Whitehurst Stone.   Phil said that the Falkners are all arrogant, that you couldn't understand any of the Falkners unless you understand that. And there's a lot of truth in it. He used to say that Judge Falkner would ride down the middle of the winding country road, going around sharp curves, expecting everybody to get out of his way. And sure enough he even lived to be killed in an automobile.

Narrator. Estelle returned from Staunton and registered as a special student at the University of Mississippi. When W. C. Handy and his band came down from Memphis to play the university dances, Estelle was the center of attention.

Emily Whitehurst Stone.   Well, the boys were just crazy about Estelle. She just looked like skin and bones, a walking skeleton, but she had whatever it takes.

Taylor McElroy.   Estelle was the most beautiful young girl I think I ever saw. And I've been looking at some pretty good-looking ones through my lifetime.

Emily Whitehurst Stone.   The girls always dreaded to go to a dance when Estelle was going to be there because the boys were around her like proverbial bees around honey. She certainly was apparently a very sexually attractive person.

Taylor McElroy.   She was the average Southern Belle, you know, just ta-ta-ta-ta-, chatter all the time and loved every good-looking boy that she ever saw. And the better they looked, the more she loved 'em.

Narrator.   One day opening a package that had come by mail she found an engagement ring sent by Cornell Franklin, seven years her senior and already graduated from Ole Miss and law school. She had accepted his proposal as frivolously

44

as she had accepted many others. Estelle turned to her parents, expecting as ever to be rescued, only to find that they not only approved, they were enthusiastic. She turned to William, urged they elope. They even took out a marriage license, but both fathers confronted him. How could he support a wife and the children that were bound to come? He could hardly support himself. Estelle found that she could not cope with two sets of determined parents and with Cornell's pleadings. Because of William's uncertain future, it was too late.

Taylor McElroy. They were literally torn away from one another's arms at that time. He was still very much in love with her and didn't want her to marry.

Finally he told himself that he hated her, that he would go away; finally he was going to as much pains to avoid her as he had been to see her . . . feeling his very heart stop when he did occasionally see her unmistakable body from a distance. Her white dress in the sun was an unbearable shimmer sloping to her body's motion as she passed from sunlight to shadow . . . leaving him to stare at the empty maw of the house in hope and despair and baffled youthful lust. (Soldiers' Pay)

Narrator. Faulkner, his world shattered, fled to New Haven to be with his friend Phil Stone.

Emily Whitehurst Stone. They were very good friends, like brothers, but they both had a passion for literature. And I'd say that was certainly the nucleus of the relationship.

Ben Wasson. Stone, for instance, gave Bill his first chance to read James Joyce with a little slim book called *Poems, Pennyeach*, which Bill admired very much. I think that Phil was the first person to call Bill's attention to many, many authors Bill otherwise wouldn't have had the opportunity of reading or knowing about.

Narrator. It was the Faulkner male tradition to look for a fight, and, as a character in a later book would say, "One doesn't want to waste a war." The five-foot, five and one-half-inch Faulkner volunteered to join the United States Army as a pilot, was rejected as too light, too short. Undeterred, he volunteered to join the Royal Air Force Canada and was accepted.

But he was still very much alive, still in Canada, still training, when suddenly the war ended. He had not been shipped overseas; he had not been commissioned; he had not even become a pilot.

Nevertheless, he came home to Oxford in the uniform of a second lieutenant, sporting wings he had purchased from a Toronto jeweler. An unfledged cadet denied fatal adventures, he invented adventures of his own. He wore a mustache, altered his speech to sound British, stuffed a

handkerchief up his sleeve, and spelled his name with a "u." He walked with a limp, confided that he wore a silver plate in his skull, complained of excruciating pains from an assortment of wounds, the consequence of a crash he claimed he suffered. His cousin said, "It got so that when Billy told you something, you didn't know if it was true or if he had just made it up."

Emily Whitehurst Stone. Bill told some lies. He told one about how when he was in Canada training for flight something happened to the airplane. He landed upside down inside the hangar. And he said, "Did you ever try to drink a bottle of whiskey when you were sitting upside down in the top of a hangar?" Well, you know, we were just agog country girls, and he said, "Well, that's what happened. I died."

All writers are congenital liars, or they wouldn't be writers in the first place.

Narrator.   Even though he had not graduated from high school, he registered at the University of Mississippi under an exception granted discharged soldiers. He spent his time writing one-act plays, an occasional review, and pursuing his interest in drawing by making illustrations for college publications, but his interest in college waned.

At this time the young man's attitude was that of most of the other young men in the world who had been around twenty-one years of age in April, 1917, even though at times he did admit to himself that he was possibly using the fact that he had been nineteen on that day as an excuse to follow the avocation he was coming more and more to know would be forever his true one: to be a tramp, a harmless possessionless vagabond. ("Mississippi")

48

Narrator.   In those youthful days he listed the requisites of a writer's trade as "whatever pleasure he can get at not too high a cost and beyond that paper, tobacco, food and a little whiskey."

He roamed through the Tallahatchie River Basin, watched people, listened to them, absorbed their dialects, observed

their varied lives. Faulkner wandered west to the Mississippi where he met the River People who he claimed fed him chocolate cake and 'possum pie. Widening his circle he traveled to the Gulf Coast, Memphis, the Delta, and New Orleans. Faulkner recorded everything he felt, everything he saw, everything he heard—stored it all, everything, to use in the stories he would write.

Round and round the mule went, setting its narrow deerlike feet delicately down in the hissing cane-path, its neck bobbing limber as a section of rubber hose in the collar, with its trace-galled flanks and flopping, lifeless ears and its half-closed eyes drowsing venomously behind pale lids, apparently asleep with the monotony of its own motion. Some Homer of the cotton fields should sing the saga of the mule and his place in the South. . . .

Father and mother he does not resemble, sons and daughters he will never have; vindictive and patient (it is a known fact that he will labor ten years willingly and patiently for you, for the privilege of kicking you once). (Sartoris)

Narrator.   In late 1921 Faulkner accepted the job Phil Stone had found for him as postmaster at the University of Mississippi in Oxford.

Ben Wasson.   Faulkner took the job because of the money. And it gave him freedom to sit back in the post office and write poetry. And his friends would gather back there. He wouldn't put up the mail and they would pound on the doors and scream to "put up the mail, put up the mail!" Faulkner paid no attention, just went on smoking his pipe. Finally, of course, the postal authorities couldn't put up with it any longer and he was ejected from the job.

George Healy.   As they filed out of the post office across the Grove towards the Falkner residence which was some 250 or 300 yards across the campus, Kincannon said, "Bill, don't you feel strange leaving this place for the last time as the lord and master? The next time we come to this post office we are going to have to treat it like a post office not a club." Bill, who didn't answer questions promptly, walked 50 or 60 paces and said, "Skeet, all my life I probably will be at the beck and call of somebody who's got money. Never again will I be at the beck and call of every son-of-a-bitch who has got two cents to buy a stamp."

Narrator.   He lost his job. But there was also good news. Phil Stone had placed a book of Faulkner's poems, *The Marble Faun*, with the Four Seas Company, a vanity press in Boston. Stone put up the four hundred dollars publication cost, and Faulkner sent in a biographical sketch stating that he was the great-grandson of Colonel W. C. Falkner, Confederate States of America, best-selling author of *The White Rose of Memphis* and *Rapid Ramblings in Europe*.

Emily Whitehurst Stone.   Monte Cooper, who was at that time the book editor for the *Commercial Appeal*, had a literary cocktail party. She invited Phil and Bill and, according to Phil, he said to Bill, "Now, Bill, we're going up there. We want to sell these books. We want to make some acquaintances. Now, I don't want you standing around like a bump on a log up against the wall all the time either. Now you get out and talk to people." Bill never would do it. But, they did go, and the party was in full swing and here came Miss Cooper sailing across the room to speak to Bill, who was standing up against the wall like a bump on a log. And she said, "You're Mr. Faulkner, aren't you?" "Yes, ma'am." "Well," she said, "I've been hearing about you, Mr. Faulkner, you've been doing some writing?" "Yes, ma'am." "Well, Mr. Faulkner, what do you think about (I don't remember who now—some author who had just come out) have you read any of his works?" "No, ma'am." "Well, what about so-and-so, have you read any of his works?" "No, ma'am." "Well, surely," she said, "you must have read thus-and-so." "No, ma'am." "Well, Mr. Faulkner, they have been telling me that you are one of the up and coming young writers. Do you mean to say you haven't read any of these books?" "Madam," he said, "did you ever hear of a whore sleepin' with a man for fun?"

Narrator.   In 1925 Faulkner left Oxford for New Orleans to catch a tramp steamer for Europe. Phil Stone had urged the trip abroad, hoping Faulkner might be discovered there, as had American expatriates Ezra Pound and Robert Frost.

Sidetracked to New Orleans, he spent time with writer Sherwood Anderson.

Anita Loos.   Sherwood said we must treat him very, very carefully because he had a silver plate in his head which he'd gotten from being some kind of war casualty. And so we all catered to this little guy, and he'd get up very late, and I would go to his bedside with a glass full of corn liquor. And that's the way he started the day.

We would walk about the city in the afternoon and talk to people. In the evenings we would meet again and sit over a bottle or two while he talked and I listened. In the forenoon I would never see him. He was secluded working. . . . I decided if that was the life of a writer, then being a writer was the thing for me. So I began to write my first book. At once I found that writing was fun. I even forgot that I hadn't seen Mr. Anderson for three weeks until he walked in my door, the first time he ever came to see me, and said, "What's wrong? Are you mad at me?" I told him I was writing a book. He said, "My God!" and walked out. (Jean Stein interview)

Outside the window New Orleans, the vieux carré, brooded in a faintly tarnished languor like an aging yet still beautiful courtesan in a smokefilled room, avid yet weary too of ardent ways.

Above banana and palm the cathedral spires soared without perspective on the hot sky. Looking through the tall pickets into Jackson Square was like looking into an aquarium. (Mosquitoes)

Narrator. He wrote sketches for a New Orleans newspaper, the first fiction he ever sold, and worked on his novel.

On July 7, 1925, after six months in New Orleans, Faulkner was finally on his way to Europe.

In Paris he frequented cafes, salons, theatres, art galleries. He explored the countryside as he had done in Mississippi. He had gone to Europe hoping to be discovered. But it didn't happen. While Frost and Hemingway were establishing their reputations, Faulkner had only a vanity book to his credit. But he was working on something that would change all that.

I have just written such a beautiful thing that I am about to bust—2000 words about the Luxembourg Gardens and death. (Letter to Maud Butler Falkner, September, 1925)

Narrator. Years later he was to recast the fragment as the ending of the novel that would bring first real notice— *Sanctuary*.

It had been a gray day, a gray summer, a gray year. On the street old men wore overcoats, and in Luxembourg Gardens as Temple and her father passed the women sat knitting shawls . . . and in the sad gloom of the chestnut trees . . . the random shouts of children, had that quality of autumn, gallant and evanescent and forlorn. (Sanctuary)

When I finished it I went to look at myself in a mirror. And I thought, Did that ugly ratty-looking face, that mixture of childishness and unreliability and sublime vanity, imagine that? But I did. (Letter to Mrs. Walter B. McLean, September, 1925)

Narrator.   By Christmas 1925 he was back in Oxford.

Always the voracious reader, his own writing reflected the writers he had read: Eliot, Conrad, Housman. He echoed the "jazz age" of F. Scott Fitzgerald, the flippant dialogue of Aldous Huxley. Not stealing, not plagiarizing, not even borrowing so much as simply trying on a variety of styles groping to evoke a voice of his own.

His first novel, *Soldiers' Pay*, a story of World War I veterans, was published in 1926 with the help of Sherwood Anderson.

Across a level moon-lit space . . . came a pure quivering chord of music wordless and far away. . . . The singing drew nearer and nearer. . . . They saw the shabby church with its canting travesty of a spire. Within it was the soft glow of kerosene serving only to make the darkness and the heat thicker, making thicker the imminence of sex after harsh labor along the mooned land; and from it welled the crooning submerged passion of the dark race. (Soldiers' Pay)

Narrator.   Encouraged by good reviews Faulkner plunged into writing his second novel, *Mosquitoes*, built around the New Orleans literary scene. When the book was published Faulkner asked the publisher, Horace Liveright, to include a dedication.

Will you please put it in for me? I made the promise some time ago, and you can lie to women, you know, but you can't break promises you make 'em. That infringes on their own province. (Letter dated January 27, 1927)

Narrator. But this time the reviews were not good. Then Faulkner remembered something Sherwood Anderson had told him when they first met:

I discovered that my own little postage stamp of native soil was worth writing about ... and that by sublimating the actual to the apocryphal I would have complete liberty to use whatever talent I might have to its absolute top. ... so I created a cosmos of my own. (Jean Stein interview)

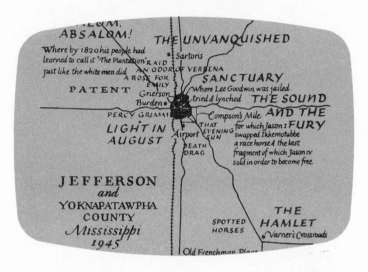

Narrator. The creation of his mythical Yoknapatawpha County gave Faulkner the opportunity on paper to be an empire builder much as his great-grandfather, the Old Colonel, had been in life.

Emily Whitehurst Stone. This woman—the visitor—said, "Bill, when you made up that story about old Mrs. So-and-So (I don't remember now who), weren't you really thinking about old lady (some lady there in Oxford—somebody, I don't remember that either)?" And Bill said, "No, I never do use anybody. I can invent much more interesting people than God ever did."

Narrator. In *Father Abraham* we encounter for the first time the Snopeses, as rapacious, as soulless, as evilly fascinating a tribe of people as can be found in all of American literature.

One afternoon he [Jody Varner] was in the store ...when at a sound behind him he turned and saw, silhouetted by the open door, a man smaller than common, in a wide hat and a frock

coat too large for him, standing with a curious planted stiffness ....
   "My name is Snopes," the man said. "I hear'd you got a farm to rent."
   "Where you been farming?" Varner said.
   "West."
   "Little anxious to get settled, ain't you?"
   The other said nothing.
   "What rent were you aiming to pay?"
   "What do you rent for?"
   "Third and fourth," Varner said. "Furnish out of the store here. No cash."
   "I'll take it," he said.
   Varner watched his caller limp stiffly across the porch and ride away.

"Who's he, Jody?"
"Name's Snopes," he said. (The Hamlet)

David Hempstead. He stopped one day on the way to lunch and said, "You know the Snopeses ship 'em to each other?" I said, "Ship what, Bill?" He said, "Other Snopeses." He said, "They just walk down to the station and they put an address card around their neck or stamp it into their lapel and mail 'em to the next town to another Snopes, and that's the way," he said, "they're all over Mississippi, all Snopeses shippin' Snopeses to other Snopeses."

Narrator. After writing twenty-five pages Faulkner abandoned *Father Abraham* and the hill people and chose instead to work on *Flags in the Dust* and the gentry. He finished the book and sent it off to Horace Liveright, who had published *Soldiers' Pay* and *Mosquitoes*, along with a gloating letter.

I have written THE book, of which those other things were but foals. I believe it is the damdest book you'll look at this year. (Undated letter [October, 1927])

Narrator. Liveright replied that while *Soldiers' Pay* was a fine book, *Mosquitoes* was not as good. *Flags in the Dust* he called "diffuse," "filled with a thousand loose ends," "disappointing."

I have a belly full of writing now, since you folks in the publishing business claim that a book like the last one I sent you is blah. I think now I'll sell my typewriter and go to work—though God knows it's sacrilege to waste that talent for idleness which I possess. (Undated letter [December, 1927])

Narrator. After numerous rejections of *Flags in the Dust*, Faulkner permitted his friend Ben Wasson to cut the manuscript by nearly half. It was later published as *Sartoris*.

He stood on a stone pedestal, in his frock coat and bareheaded, one leg slightly advanced. . . . His head was lifted a little in that gesture of haughty pride which repeated itself generation after generation with a fateful fidelity, his back to the world and his carven eyes gazing out across the valley where his railroad ran, and the blue changeless hills beyond, and beyond that, the ramparts of infinity itself. (Sartoris)

Narrator. In 1928 Faulkner began reworking a piece about the Compson children, a short story he called "Twilight." But the fragment expanded beyond the short story.

When I began the book I had no plan at all. I wasn't even writing a book. Previous to it I had written three novels, with

progressively decreasing ease and pleasure. . . . One day it sud-
denly seemed as if a door had clapped silently and forever
to between me and all publishers' addresses and booklists and
I said to myself, Now I can write. Now I can make myself a
vase like that which the old Roman kept at his bedside and
wore the rim slowly away with kissing it. (Unpublished introduction to *The Sound and the Fury,* August, 1933)

Ben Wasson. He said, "Read this, Bud. It's a real son of a
bitch." I opened it and it was a title page which read "*The
Sound and the Fury* by William Faulkner."

Narrator. One of Faulkner's early teachers had been
Miss Annie Chandler. She and her sister took care of their
brother, a man in his thirties with the mind of a child, who
used to spend his days following the fence that surrounds
this yard. Often young William passing this fence could see
the brother.

Benjy was an idiot, spent most of his time with a negro nurse
in the pasture, until the pasture was deeded in the County Re-
corder's office as sold. Was fond of his sister, could always

be quieted indoors when placed where he could watch firelight. Was gelded by process of law, when and (assumed) why, since the little girl he scared probably made a good story out of it when she got over being scared. (Letter to Malcolm Cowley, October 27, 1945)

Narrator.   Faulkner shifted his characters through different layers of time from when they were children to years later when Caddy is gone. Remembered time was one with the present. It was a style of writing that even the most sophisticated reader was bound to find difficult. He described the effort as "almost like trying to write the Lord's Prayer on the head of a pin."

When *The Sound and the Fury* was published, the critics' response was instantaneous. Many said it was a book with the qualities of greatness; one even called it "worthy of the attention of a Euripides." But it would be years and years before *The Sound and the Fury* had any sizable sales.

Albert Erskine.   It took sixteen years to sell out the three thousand copies printed.

Narrator. Prior to the publication of *The Sound and the Fury*, with very little to his name, Faulkner announced he would marry Estelle, home from China with two children and divorced from Cornell Franklin. The announcement came as no great surprise. Estelle had once written a friend that while Cornell had his lovers in Shanghai, hers was in Oxford.

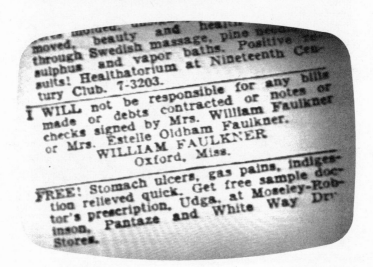

moved, beauty and health through Swedish massage, pine needle, sulphus and vapor baths. Positive results! Healthatorium at Nineteenth Century Club. 7-3203.

I WILL not be responsible for any bills made or debts contracted or notes or checks signed by Mrs. William Faulkner or Mrs. Estelle Oldham Faulkner.
WILLIAM FAULKNER
Oxford, Miss.

FREE! Stomach ulcers, gas pains, indigestion relieved quick. Get free sample doctor's prescription, Udga, at Moseley-Robinson, Pantaze and White Way Drug Stores.

Estelle had been a rich man's indulged wife who had acquired a whole set of new values, ones Faulkner couldn't afford. Several years later he would put a notice in the local paper for all to read disclaiming any debts she incurred.

Faulkner had changed too. He had become the writer he had always promised to be, accustomed to living and working alone, being responsible to and for no one—able to pick up and go with his manuscript in his pocket whenever he wanted.

Jill Faulkner Summers.   He didn't really care about people, and he certainly didn't care what people felt about him. But he would never willingly offend anybody. He never would willingly hurt someone. But still, he didn't really care about people. I think he cared about me. But, I also think I could have gotten in his way and he would have walked on me.

Narrator.   There was quickly evidence that the prospects for the newlyweds would not be good. As the years passed they would grow further and further apart. One evening during the summer on the Gulf Coast Estelle, dressed in one of her exotic Shanghai gowns, walked into the water and tried to drown herself. But she would outlive Faulkner by a decade.

Marc Connelly.   His wife was a very nervous girl who occasionally had some kind of slips of mental processes, of thinking, and so on. And I don't know what she did, but it was something with which Bill was obviously familiar. And quite objectively, without a bit of reproachment in it, he looked at his wife and reached out and slapped her face very hard which, undoubtedly, was physically painful to her. She went right back to completely normal conduct, and Bill, without any apologies or anything else, continued whatever he had been talking about. It was a strange sort of thing, because it was corrective without being a punishment. Then and there, I thought, this is a very extraordinary man.

Narrator.   To support his new family Faulkner found a job working nights at the university power generating station.

He claimed he wrote *As I Lay Dying* in six weeks while

sitting in a coal bunker, using the bottom of an overturned wheelbarrow as a writing desk.

As I Lay Dying is the story of the Bundren family, of Addie, her husband and children, of how when Addie died they hauled her corpse to the county seat in Jefferson to fulfill her wish to be buried with her own people—a rejection, even in death, of her husband and children.

I could just remember how my father used to say that the reason for living was to get ready to stay dead for a long time. And when I would have to look at them day after day, each with his and her secret and selfish thought, and blood strange to each other blood and strange to mine, and think that this seemed to be the only way I could get ready to stay dead, I would hate my father for having ever planted me.

. . . I knew that living was terrible and that this was the answer to it . . . that we had had to use one another by words like spiders dangling by their mouths from a beam, swinging and twisting and never touching, and that only through the blows of the switch could my blood and their blood flow as one stream. (As I Lay Dying)

Narrator. In 1931 Faulkner scraped up enough money to make a down payment on the old Shegog place. Set amid several acres of isolated woodland, the imposing old house had been built in the 1840s.

Dean Faulkner Wells. Pappy made her up—the family ghost, the daughter of the Shegog family. She was young and lovely when the Yankees came to Oxford, and she fell head over heels in love with a Yankee soldier and wanted to marry him. Papa Shegog said, "You may not do this." So this broken-hearted girl climbed up to the top balcony, jumped off and landed on the steps, and broke her neck. She is buried down the driveway under the magnolia tree. We believed every word of it. I did until I was a grown woman—I believed it.

Narrator.   He renamed it Rowan Oak after the British tree of good luck, and what little time he could spare from writing he spent working on the house. It would be both a private place to work and a symbol of his growing status as a writer in the same cast as the Old Colonel. Over the years his renovations were a constant financial drain.

Phil Mullen.   He was a plantation man. That's what he was. That's what he was trying to do. He was trying to live like his great-grandfather did in all his ways. Cured his own ham. He had a grandfather who had written *The White Rose of Memphis*, built a railroad, killed a man in a duel, commanded two regiments during the Civil War—why, you would want to be one too.

Jill Faulkner Summers.   Everybody in Oxford had remembered that Pappy's father ran a livery stable. He had
lived in this house up not too far from the livery stable.
So this was just a way of thumbing his nose at Oxford, you
know.

Phil Mullen.   One Sunday morning Bill and his drinking
buddies—that is, some of the town's most prominent citizens—had gotten together for a party. Maybe it was a wind-
up to the party the night before, but they were all dressed
up in costumes. They were knights and so forth, and they
had the Negroes dressed up in livery. They had a huntin'
breakfast and had their picture taken. And then they rode
mules and so forth downtown around the square just as
church was breaking up so everybody could see 'em. He
just didn't care what the bluenoses thought of him.

Jill Faulkner Summers.   He could be extremely court-
ly. No one could look quite as elegant as Pappy could when
he was dressed for the occasion. And you didn't feel em-
barrassed when he bowed. You could imagine if he had
a cloak on he could swing it off and put it in a mud puddle
and you walk on it.

Narrator.   To meet his new debts and obligations he
wrote a book deliberately aimed at the buying public. Written with care and power, it was a book filled with violence,
a book he hoped would land him on the best seller list.
But the publisher returned it replying "Good God, I can't
print that. We'd both be in jail." Heavily revised in form
and style, *Sanctuary* was published in 1931.

Robert Penn Warren.   In *Sanctuary* he first struck on
one of his great ideas, dehumanized modern man. Popeye
is modern man. Popeye the machine. The man is afraid of
nature. An owl goes by, and he scrambles to grab onto
his companion, you see, to protect himself. "That's just an
owl," says Benbow. And then he and Benbow listen to the

Carolina wren. He said, "It's a bird. But you wouldn't rec-
ognize a bird unless you saw it on a plate in a hotel and it
cost four dollars."

Narrator.   The public loved it. In three weeks it sold
more copies than *The Sound and the Fury* and *As I Lay Dying*
had in two years. Then the publisher went broke. But not
before Faulkner's writing had caught the discerning eye of
the motion picture agent, Sam Marx. Before the year was
out Faulkner astounded his father and home town by earn-
ing five hundred dollars a week by writing what they called
"moom pictures."

Sam Marx.   I told him I had an assignment for him, and
before I got to it, he said, "Well, I want you to know
that really the only movies I'd like to work on are either
for Mickey Mouse or for newsreels."

Marc Connelly.   He was invited into the office of Mr.
Irving Thalberg, who was the crown prince of Hollywood
at that time, a man of enormous energy and pretty con-
ventional tastes, who asked Bill if he was at all familiar
with the operation of MGM. And Bill, of course, had a

marvelous ploy. He was forever carrying a pipe, and when he was asked that, he put the pipe in his mouth, blew out some smoke, which gave him time to phrase his question. He said, "Well, now, I don't think I am. Do you make the Mickey Mouse brand?"

Narrator.   In 1932 the motion picture director Howard Hawks bought the film rights to Faulkner's short story, "Turnabout," published in the *Saturday Evening Post*.

Howard Hawks.   I sent him a wire and asked him if he would like to do the script on it and sent him a check. He arrived, smoking a pipe, and I said, "My name's Hawks," and he said, "I read it on the check." He didn't say any-thing and I talked, and the more I talked the madder I got because he didn't say anything. And I talked for about forty minutes, telling him how I wanted to handle his story. I said, "Well, that's all." He got up and, "O.K.," I said, "where are you going?" He said, "Well, you wanted me to write it, didn't you?" And I said, "Yes, but I'd like to know you a little bit better." I said, "Would you like a drink?" He said, "I certainly would." We woke up the next morning in a little motel in Culver City, and he was fishing cigarette stubs out of a mint julep. He was showing me how to make 'em. He said, "I'll see you in about five days." He came in five days later and he had a perfect script, just a beautiful piece of work.

Narrator.   Faulkner's times in Hollywood were marked by apocryphal stories about him which over the years have become legend.

Ben Maddow.   You all know the famous story of Faulkner asking his producer whether he could work at home.

Marc Connelly.   The producer says, "You come in everyday to the studio?" Mr. Faulkner says, "Yes." I suppose he didn't use the pipe for that answer. He said, "Perhaps rather than come into the studio every day you'd like to write at home?" Bill says, "Yes, that would be very desirable."

Lauren Bacall.   Faulkner said, "Do you mind if I work at home?" And the producer said, "Oh, no—no, not at all." So only a couple weeks went by, and there was no word

from Faulkner. The producer called his hotel and asked to speak to Faulkner and Faulkner had checked out. He didn't know what the hell was going on. He finally realized that when Faulkner said he was going to work at home, he was going to work in Mississippi.

Sam Marx.   Well, that story, which, of course, I hear constantly, is not true. Really it's not. I was in charge of the writers. He would have had to come to me. It never happened.

Narrator.   While Faulkner was in Hollywood, struggling to make a living, his books were going unread in the United States, but his reputation in France was growing steadily, mainly because of the excellent translations by Professor Maurice Coindreau.

Maurice Coindreau.   The first novel I translated was *As I Laying Dying*. That book just fascinated the critics and was very well received. Later, while I was translating *The Sound and the Fury*, I went to Hollywood and lived at Faulkner's house for about ten days. He was working for the studio and would come back at night and say, "Well, now what

is the problem this time?" So I showed him all the different things that troubled me, and he gave me a great deal of information. The book was a tremendous success in France.

Narrator.   Faulkner needed money and had every reason to expect that his new novel, *Light in August*, published in 1932, would sell as well as *Sanctuary*.

*The next day he lay again all day long on his cot in the cabin. . . .
'Better blow,' he thought. 'Not give her the chance to turn me
out of the cabin too. That much, anyway. No white woman
ever did that. Only a nigger woman ever give me the air, turned
me out.' So he lay on the cot, smoking, waiting for sunset.
Through the open door he watched the sun slant and lengthen
and turn copper. Then the copper faded into lilac, into the fading
lilac of full dusk. He could hear the frogs then, and fireflies
began to drift across the open frame of the door, growing bright-
er as the dusk faded. Then he rose. He owned nothing but the
razor; when he put that into his pocket, he was ready to travel
one mile or a thousand, wherever the street of the imperceptible
corners should choose to run again. Yet when he moved, it was
toward the house. (Light in August)*

INTERMISSION

Narrator. But despite excellent reviews, *Light in August*
did not sell. Driven by his mounting debts, Faulkner wel-
comed the chance to work in Hollywood for ready cash.

Ben Wasson. Today people say that Faulkner hated Hollywood. I don't think he actually did hate Hollywood. It
was fashionable among writers at the time to say they hated
the place. But most of them didn't mean it, as evidenced
by how long they stayed and how often they came back
for jobs.

Howard Hawks. Faulkner and I were going hunting
down in Imperial Valley after doves, and Clark Gable called
up and said, "What are you doing?" I said, "We're going
hunting. I'm going hunting with a fella called Bill Faulkner."
And he said, "Can I go?" I said, "Yeah, if you can get over
here in half an hour." So he came charging over, and we
got in the station wagon. We had a couple of drinks on the
way down. We started talking, and I don't know why the

conversation got into literature and Gable said, "Who do you think are the good writers, Mr. Faulkner?" Faulkner says, "Thomas Mann, Willa Cather, John Dos Passos, Ernest Hemingway, and myself." And Gable looked kinda funny and said, "Do you write, Mr. Faulkner?" Faulkner says, "Yes, what do you do, Mr. Gable?"

Jill Faulkner Summers.   Pappy didn't like going to Hollywood. He dreaded it, but he did go out there when he simply had to make money. Once he got there I think he had a good time. And I think he enjoyed the people he met because Pappy didn't like ordinary people.

V. P. Ferguson.   Met him altogether by chance thanks to his stepson, a tremendous character named Malcolm Franklin. In fact, they were all characters. In fact, I was myself at that time a character. They all were, and I thought I was meeting something there. That was my first impression of William Faulkner.

Narrator.   This time when Faulkner returned from his picture assignment there was money enough to buy himself an airplane.

79

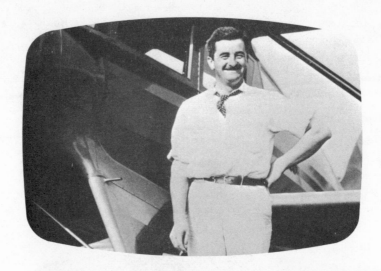

And then a year later a girl child was born. Faulkner's joy
was limitless. Estelle thought he would be disappointed, but
he told her there were too many Faulkner boys already.
They named her Jill, and as soon as he could he took her
for plane rides to share his early dreams.

Jill Faulkner Summers.   The planes always had a very
special part in his life. The dashing aviator, you know, with

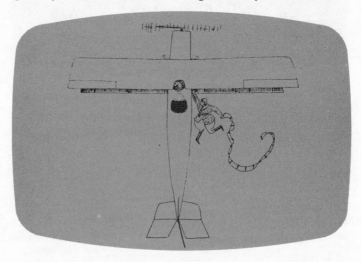

the scarf around the neck flowing off in the breeze, and what have you.

Narrator.   During the Depression Faulkner helped his brothers by paying for flying lessons and gave Dean the plane to help earn a living for him and his new wife. Faulkner's avid interest in flying led to his writing *Pylon*, a book about the barnstorming pilots who moved from airport to airport giving stunt shows, engaging in races, showing the locals their farms from a thousand or so feet, all done to support their families and themselves. Suddenly, tragically, his life seemed to draw from the book itself.

. . . it was not the crash that he heard: it was a single long exhalation of human breath as though the microphone had reached out and caught that too out of all the air which people had ever breathed. . . . it was as though all the faces, all the past twenty-four hours' victories and defeats and hopes and renunciations and despairs, had been blasted completely out of his life as if they had actually been the random sheets of that organ to which he dedicated his days, caught momentarily upon one senseless member of the scarecrow which he resembled, and then blown away . . . he saw the aeroplane lying on its back,

the undercarriage projecting into the air rigid and delicate and motionless as the legs of a dead bird. (Pylon)

Narrator.   In March, 1935, *Pylon* was published. That November, Dean crashed in the plane Faulkner had given him. Faulkner never lost the feeling that he was responsible for the death of his brother. Much as Roger Shumann had accepted responsibility for Laverne and her unborn child in the novel, Faulkner did the same for Dean's widow and the child she carried.

Louise Meadows.   Oh, I think it was the worst thing that ever happened in his life. And in addition to missing his brother whom he loved so much, he felt responsible because he had given Dean the plane. So he felt a strong feeling of guilt that I think he fought an awfully long time to get over, if he ever did. I remember one morning we were eating breakfast, just the two of us, and I said, "Oh, I didn't sleep last night, I had such horrible dreams." And he said, "Did you dream about the accident?" I said, "Yes, I did, I dreamed it all over." And he said, "Love, I have done it every night since it happened."

Narrator.   The epitaph he wrote for Dean was the same one he had given to Lieutenant John Sartoris in *Flags in the Dust*.

'I bare him on eagles' wings and brought him unto Me.'

Narrator.   In an effort to deal with his guilt and grief, Faulkner plunged into finishing the first of his novels to be published by Random House.

David Hempstead.   When I went in the next day to see him and return the manuscript, exhausted, I told him what I thought of it, which was that it was great, and he said, "You liked it?" I said, "Yes, more than that." He said, "Well, I think it's the best novel yet written by an American."

Narrator.   The novel was *Absalom, Absalom!*, published in 1936. Faulkner had labored long on this complex and brilliant novel.

It seems that this demon—his name was Sutpen—(Colonel Sutpen)—Colonel Sutpen. Who came out of nowhere and without warning upon the land with a band of strange niggers and built

*a plantation—(Tore violently a plantation, Miss Rosa Coldfield
says)—tore violently. And married her sisten Ellen and begot
a son and a daughter which—(Without gentleness begot, Miss
Rosa Coldfield says)—without gentleness. Which should have
been the jewels, his pride, and the comfort of his old age, only—
(Only they destroyed him or something or he destroyed them or
something. And died.)—and died. Without regret, Miss Rosa
Coldfield says—(Save by her) Yes, save by her. (And by Quentin
Compson) Yes. And by Quentin Compson. (Absalom, Absalom!)*

Narrator.   *Absalom, Absalom!* is one of the world's great
novels, but the book did not, nor did the three which fol-
lowed, earn enough money to support Faulkner, his family,
and his dependents, at one time seventeen in number.

Jill Faulkner Summers.   Pappy had no sense of money
at all—never did. And he was the easiest touch. He always
had several families completely dependent upon him. Anyone could come to him with a hard luck story, and he would
accept it and put his hand in his pocket whether there
was anything there or not and cheerfully give them whatever he had.

*Beginning at the age of thirty I, an artist, a sincere one and
of the first class, who should be free even of his own economic
responsibilities and with no moral conscience at all, began to
become the sole provider, principal and partial support—food,
shelter, heat, clothes, medicine, kotex, school fees, toilet paper
and picture shows—of my mother, my brother's wife and
children, another brother's widow and child, a wife of my own and
two step children, my own child; I inherited my father's debts and
his dependents, white and black without inheriting yet from
anyone one inch of land or one stick of furniture or one cent of
money . . . I am 42 years old and have already paid for four
funerals and will certainly pay for one more and in all likelihood
two more beside that, provided none of the people in mine or my
wife's family my superior in age outlive me before I ever come to
my own.* (Letter to Robert K. Haas, May, 1940)

Narrator.   In January, 1940, Faulkner explained a delay in
editing proofs of *The Hamlet*, the first of the Snopes trilogy.

*Galley being returned today. Sorry I am late with it, but the
old hundred-year-old matriarch who raised me died suddenly . . .
so I have had little of heart or time either for work.*
(Letter to Robert K. Haas, February 5, 1940)

Narrator.   In his next book Faulkner wrote this dedication:

TO MAMMY

CAROLINE BARR

Mississippi
[1840–1940]

*Who was born in slavery and who gave to my family
a fidelity without stint or calculation of recompense
and to my childhood an immeasurable devotion and
love*

To Mammy I came to represent the head of that family to which she had given a half century of fidelity and devotion but the relationship between us never came to that of master and servant. . . . She assumed cares and griefs which were not even her cares and griefs. . . . From her I learned to tell the truth, to refrain from waste, to be considerate of the weak and respectful to age. (Eulogy at funeral of Caroline Barr, February 4, 1940)

M. R. Phillips. One morning we was down there, she

come in and I's standing round the back door, and she walked up and said, "Boy, where's Billy?" I says, "He upstairs, I reckon, and he hasn't come down." And Miz 'Stelle, she's upstairs in the hall and hear me and she says, "He's in the bathroom, Mammy Calley." She says, "I don't care where that boy's at, I give him a bath before he give hisself a bath." And she just kep' on walkin'. Miz 'Stelle said, "You can't go in there, he's in the bathtub." And he says, "Let Mammy Calley alone, don't bother her," and she come on to the door and opened it and he's settin' in the tub. He said, "What's the matter, Mammy Calley?" "I ain't got no coffee and I ain't got no snuff." And he says to Miz 'Stelle, "Go down there and tell the cook to fix Mammy Calley some coffee right now." "What if we don't have it?" He said, "I said fix Mammy Calley some coffee now and give it to her." She come on down and got her coffee, and he got the chauffeur and the butler and sent them to town with Mammy Calley to get whatever she wanted and carry her home. She didn't worry 'bout anything.

Narrator. Through the years he returned to Hollywood again and again. He was rarely happy there, ached to return to Mississippi. His dilemma deepened when agent William

Herndon, acting with Faulkner's power of attorney, committed him to a long-term contract at Warner Brothers Studios. The brothers Warner could drop their end of the contract at the slightest whim while Faulkner could not escape the binding deal. The studio owned film rights to everything he would write for the next seven years. Jack Warner, studio head, liked to boast that he had the world's best writer working for peanuts.

Buzz Bezzerides.   I guess Warner thought that if he gave

these dog assignments to these wonderful writers, somehow they'd turn a dog into a silk purse, and it never worked.

Lauren Bacall.   He wrote some scenes for *The Big Sleep*.
The first scene that he wrote, I remember, he brought
down to the set, very, very pleased with himself and gave
it to Howard. It was a two-page scene, single spaced, for
one character to speak, which is impossible, totally impos-

sible, on the screen. It was not a scene between people. It was one. So Howard kind of passed it to Bogey, and Bogey looked at it. Howard kind of chuckled, and Bogey kind of chuckled.

David Hempstead.   Customarily a writer might do five to ten pages a day and think this was a phenomenal achievement. Bill could do forty or fifty. Now, maybe you couldn't use it because the speeches would be four pages long apiece, but the amount of work that he'd turn out was enough to outrage the militant members of the Screen Writers Guild.

Narrator.   Faulkner had written a screen play of Stephen Longstreet's novel, *Stallion Road*, which the studio rejected.

Stephen Longstreet.   We wrote another one. He didn't put his name on it. Maybe you've seen the damn thing—it's on late hour television. We were promised Bogart and Bacall as the stars of the picture. We ended up with Ronald Reagan and Alexis Smith. And the picture is really a rather bad picture. New York critics said, "If you're a horse, you will like this picture." So Faulkner sent a telegram to Ronald Reagan saying, "My horse didn't like it."

Narrator.   Trapped in a repressive contract, far from home, and mostly broke despite having a job, Faulkner resorted to the only escape available to him.

Jill Faulkner Summers.   He simply drank. If you left him alone, he would drink for days, sometimes as long as a week or ten days. And when he was ready to sober up, he would. No one else could sober him up. There was no such thing as stopping Pappy from drinking. He drank until he was ready to quit.

Victoria Black.   When I was 16 I couldn't quite cope with it, and Pappy understood that I couldn't cope because he said, "Call Malcolm and get him to take me up to Byhalia." Two days later he was back sitting on the front porch when I drove in and he said, "Vick Pick, I knew you needed help—you couldn't handle it." So even in his drunken stupor he did have the sensitivity and the heart to know that I couldn't take it.

David Hempstead.   I never knew anyone who would drink until he was unconscious and then get conscious just long enough to do the same thing all over again. I'd say, "I don't understand why or how you can stay alive." He said, "Well, Dave, there's a lot of nourishment in an acre of corn."

Jill Faulkner Summers.   I remember once, it was just before my birthday and I knew that Pappy was getting ready to start on one of these bouts. I went to him—the only time I ever did—and said, "Please don't start drinking." And he was already well on his way, and he turned to me and said, "You know, no one remembers Shakespeare's child." I never asked him again.

Narrator.   Faulkner's Hollywood years were among his worst, writing not for the writing but for the money. "Going whoring" he called it.

Albert Erskine.   There was talk about story conferences in Hollywood and how terrible they were. And the young writer said, "Mr. Faulkner, how could you stand that?" Bill said, "I would just keep saying under my breath, 'They're gonna pay me Saturday, they gonna pay me Saturday, they gonna pay me Saturday.'"

Narrator.   For years he appealed for release from his contract. And for years Jack Warner refused. Then one day Faulkner just walked out and went home to Mississippi—to hell with Jack Warner and Hollywood. Now he was home to work, to visit the Square, to play with his daughter, to sail his boat, to hunt with his cronies.

Robert Evans.   Bill Faulkner was a fine, fine hunter. He
was a quiet hunter. Fact of the business he was a pretty
quiet man in camp. You didn't never hear no hoorahing
and storming and all this, that, and the other going on from
·Bill. Now, he would laugh and talk and tell little stories.

Jill Faulkner Summers.   Pappy loved the outdoors. He
loved to be outside. He loved to walk for hours and hours
and hours. And he liked hunting because he liked to be in
the woods. He didn't like killing things. I think that he
killed only when he was shamed into it—that's not the
word I wanted—but when it was unavoidable because we'd
go bird shooting and he liked to watch the dogs work.
He didn't care whether we had a good covey rise or whether he'd get something to kill or not. And he very seldom
brought deer back from the deer hunts that he went on
down in the Delta.

Howard Hawks.   He was a very good shot. If I'd say
"good shot" to him, he would say, "Is Hemingway better
than I am?" And I'd say, "Yes." He'd keep still for awhile.
And he'd say, "In what way is he better?" And I'd say, "He
does more bird shooting than you do." "You mean, is he

really awful good?" I'd say, "No, my wife could beat him anytime." But Bill was a different kind of a sportsman. Ernest was always trying to prove what a man he was. Bill didn't give a damn about proving that—just enjoying himself and being with people that he liked.

Narrator. When he was small, hunting had been an important part of his life—a ritual marking a boy's passage to manhood. Some of the finest stories he wrote were about the big woods and hunting.

Malcolm Cowley. Think, for example, of Ike McCaslin, a boy of twelve, setting out to see the bear. He goes out and hunts for him all day for three days running.

It was as if the boy had already divined what his senses and intellect had not encompassed yet: that doomed wilderness whose edges were being constantly and punily gnawed at by men with plows and axes who feared it because it was wilderness, men myriad and nameless even to one another in the land where the old bear had earned a name, and through which ran not even a mortal beast but an anachronism indomitable and invincible out of an old dead time, a phantom, epitome and apotheosis

of the old wild life which the littly puny humans swarmed and hacked at in fury of abhorrence and fear, like pygmies about the ankles of a drowsing elephant;—the old bear, solitary, indomitable, and alone; widowered childless, and absolved of mortality—old Priam reft of his old wife and outlived all his sons. ("The Bear," in *The Big Woods*)

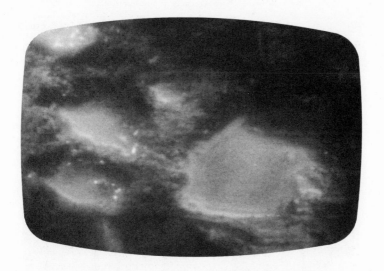

Malcolm Cowley. At the end of the third day Sam Fathers says to him, "It's the gun." So he leaves the gun behind and goes out to look for the bear. And then he himself has the feeling that no, it was not only the gun, but also the knife and the compass and the stick that he had. Those manmade objects would keep the bear from showing himself. So he hangs the compass and the knife on a bush, leans the stick against the bush and then becomes totally lost in the wilderness for the first time. He decides to make a big circle. He can't find his footprints again, so he makes a circle in the other direction and then he stands still to think for a moment, comes out in a swampy glade, looks down and there are the paw prints of the enormous bear with the wounded paw, the three-toed paw, there gradually filling with water. He looks up and there the bear suddenly materializes out of the wilderness. And that isn't magic? That's the sort of magic you find in a fairy story. And that quality one finds in story after story by Faulkner, and in novel after novel until you say "yes, this is genius, truly this is genius."

And now the young man, middleaged now or anyway middle-aging, is back home where they who altered the swamps

*and forests of his youth, have now altered the face of the earth
itself; what he remembered as dense river bottom jungle and
rich farm land, is now an artificial lake twenty-five miles long. . . .
Home again, his native land; He was born of it and his bones
will sleep in it; loving it even while hating some of it: the
river jungle and the bordering hills where still a child he had
ridden behind his father on a horse . . . where he hunted alone
when he got big enough to be trusted with a gun, now the
bottom of a muddy lake being raised gradually and steadily every
year by another layer of beer cans and bottle caps and lost
bass plugs.* ("Mississippi")*

Narrator.   The years between 1929 and 1942 had been
Faulkner's most productive. But by the early '40s all but
one of his books were out of print in the United States.
He was not being read, not being bought. His financial plight
was at its worst.

*I have all my original manuscripts, most of them in handwriting.
I will sell or mortgage . . . . $6,000.00 is what we have to raise.
. . . If I could have $10,000 to pay off my debts, take care of
my responsibilities. . . . I still have some money left, though not*

enough to buy my freedom. . . . I tried last summer to explain to you about $1,600 additional 1937 income tax . . . my income had been reduced about 95% . . . sue and be damned . . . . you may even get an autographed book. That will be worth a damn sight more than my autograph on a check dated ten months from now. (Letters, 1939)

Shelby Foote.   It was a time of great distress for him. I think that he had strong evidence that he had failed as a writer who was going to survive. After all, his books were out. I don't think he had any doubt about his work, but he did have some doubt about whether that work was going to last or not since the evidence was that it wouldn't.

Narrator.   But still he wrote, he always wrote. To buy time to write his novels, to keep his debts at bay, Faulkner turned out commercial stories, even though by contract they belonged to Warner Brothers. He turned them out swiftly and sent them to editor after editor. But they rarely bought, and the public, as far as Faulkner's work was concerned, seemed totally indifferent. Even so, he was being read by many of the world's intellectuals.

Michel Gresset. Faulkner was then heralded by several French writers who were in their greatest days. I'm thinking, of course, of Malraux, even LeBeau, who was not a negligible writer, and, of course, Sartre. And then later Camus. With these three, Malraux, Sartre, and Camus, you have the greatest French writers of that part of the century in this country.

Carvel Collins. Camus and the other Frenchmen in the

underground, with Germans occupying Paris and much of France, turned to Faulkner. And they are the ones who created the boom that now exists in Faulkner's popularity in academia. It was the French who began it. And I can't think that Camus and his colleagues in the underground, with the enemy there, were interested in any author just because he was telling historical and sociological facts about a section of some foreign country. I think they saw that he had based it solidly on home stuff and then was building on the larger philosophical thing which they could share.

Narrator.   Malcolm Cowley proposed reshaping Faulkner's work into a chronological order.

Malcolm Cowley.   On August 9, 1945, I wrote, "Dear Faulkner: It's gone through, there will be a Viking Portable Faulkner, and it seems a very good piece of news to me. . . . It won't be a very big transaction from the financial point of view. The Viking Portables have only a moderate sale— the Hemingway I edited sold about 30,000 copies [in the first year] and they thought that was extra good. But the reason the book pleases me is that it gives me a chance to present your work as a whole, at a time when every one of your books except *'Sanctuary'*—and I'm not even sure about that—is out of print. The result should be a better sale for your new books and a bayonet prick in the ass of Random House to reprint the others." The bayonet prick worked right away.

Narrator.   Cowley's book, a selection of stories and fragments from Faulkner's novels, plus Faulkner's detailed map of Yoknapatawpha County, appeared in 1946. *The Portable Faulkner* helped him gain the wide audience in America that he had always enjoyed in France. But he was still missing from the best seller list.

Malcolm Cowley.   I didn't know at the time how far down Faulkner was inside his head. I've just found a letter to his agent: "My books have never sold, are out of print. The labor in the creation of my apocryphal county of my life even if I have a few things yet to say to add to it, will never make a living for me. I don't have enough sure judgment about trash to be able to write it with 50% success. Could I do some sort of editorial work or some sort of hack writing at home where living won't cost me as much as now?"

Tennessee Williams. He looked slowly up, and his eyes were so incredibly sad that I, being a somewhat emotional person, began to cry uncontrollably. I have never seen such sad eyes on a human face.

Narrator. Suddenly, Faulkner's celebrity soared. MGM sent a motion picture crew to Oxford to film Faulkner's new novel, *Intruder in the Dust*. Though the townspeople by and large still ignored the book, they flocked to be extras in the movie. On the surface, *Intruder in the Dust* is about the trial of a black man accused of murdering a white. In reality, it's the story of a black man who refuses to act like a "nigger."

Segregation is going, whether we like it or not. . . . Shall seg-
regation be abolished by force, or shall it be abolished by choice,
by us in the South who will have to bear the burden of it?
It is a sad commentary on human nature that it is much easier,
simpler, much more fun and excitement, to be against some-
thing you can see, like a black skin, than to be for some-
thing you can only believe in as a principle, like justice and
fairness and (in the long view) the continuation of individual
freedom and liberty. (Letter to David Kirk, March 8, 1956)

Narrator.   Though Faulkner was beginning to find relief
from his financial burdens, his personal life with Estelle continued to be troubled. That winter he met a pretty, 21
year-old aspiring writer from Memphis, Joan Williams.

Joan Williams.   He had come to a point where he just
simply was lonesome. And he needed somebody. He
said, "I have to have somebody suddenly for the first
time in my life that I feel that I am doing the writing for.
I've got to be doing it for somebody." He said that he'd
always been the cat who walked by himself and that

this didn't exist any longer. And in a letter when he was working on *Requiem*, he said, "So I do need you. Not coddling but affection, warmth. So I can believe again that work is worthwhile and do it. Sympathy. 'Fun' in a word, maybe. To talk fantasy and nonsense and good sense and truth and to equals, to believe in the same things, believe that the same things are true and important and worth believing in. Damn it, I want somebody to give to. All anybody wants here is just money which like this I can't earn because I can't work because of no warmth and affection or sympathy. None to say yes, yes to me and I want to say yes, yes, yes to the dear face in return."

Jill Faulkner Summers. Pappy liked ladies, liked women, you know, plain and simple. I think that Joan was important because she was writing and it appealed to something in Pappy to have a protégé.

Narrator.   Joan Williams was not the only woman Faulkner knew. Meta Carpenter, a Hollywood script girl from Mississippi, knew Faulkner for eighteen years.

Shelby Foote. It was something that had gone from his life, and he was attempting to recover it, I suppose. I've seen him call on a young lady with a large bunch of violets in his hand. That seemed to me a nice thing to do— not foolish at all.

Jill Faulkner Summers. I think that probably Pappy's idea of women—ladies—always revolved a great deal around Granny. She was just a very determined, tiny old lady that Pappy adored. Pappy admired that so much in Granny and he didn't find it in my mother and I don't think he ever found it in anybody. I think that maybe all of these including my mother were, just second place. It's difficult to say.

If you are a fool enough to marry at all, keep the first one and stay as far away from her as much as you can, with the hope of some day outliving her. At least you will be safe then from any other one marrying you—which is bound to happen if you ever divorce her. Apparently man can be cured of drugs, drink, gambling, biting his nails, and picking his nose, but not of marrying. (Letter to Malcolm Cowley, September 20, 1945)

Yet this art, which has no place in Southern life, is almost the sum total of the Southern artist. It is his breath, blood, flesh, all. . . . We seem to try . . . to draw a savage indictment of the contemporary scene or to escape from it into a makebelieve region of swords and magnolias and mockingbirds which per- haps never existed anywhere . . . the writer unconsciously writes into every line and phrase his violent despairs and rages and frustrations or his violent prophesies of still more violent hopes. . . . I do not believe there lives the Southern writer who can say without lying that writing is any fun to him. Perhaps we do not want it to be. (Unpublished introduction to *The Sound and the Fury*)

I decline to accept the end of man. It is easy enough to say that man is immortal simply because he will endure: that when the last ding-dong of doom has clanged and faded from the last worthless rock hanging tideless in the last red and dying evening, that even then there will still be one more sound: that of his puny inexhaustible voice, still talking. . . . The poet's voice need not merely be the record of man, it can be one of the props, the pillars to help him endure and prevail. (Nobel Prize Acceptance Speech)

Narrator.   The world finally recognized William Faulkner's genius when he was awarded the 1949 Nobel Prize for literature. The announcement came on November 10, 1950, fifteen years to the day of the death of his brother Dean.

Mrs. William Bradley.   When he came for the Nobel Prize it was amazing the number of young writers and young readers who came and who wanted to meet him. And his publisher Gallimard gave a cocktail party for him, and it was very touching really, all those youngsters coming. I've never seen that happen.

Phyllis Cerf Wagner. They all began to tell us—in this tiny little hotel room—his adventures in getting the Nobel Prize. And suddenly, in the midst of the conversation, he said, "By the way, Bennett, that full dress suit you rented for me, I think I'd like to keep that suit." And I said, "Bill, what are you going to do with it?" "Well," he said, "I might stuff it and put it in the living room in Mississippi and charge people to come in and see it, or I might rent it out, but, I want that suit." So Random House had to buy it.

Joseph Blotner. In my view Faulkner is the best novelist that this country has produced. For several reasons: I think he belongs certainly in the company of Hawthorne, Melville, and James because of his technical accomplishments, but also because of the way in which his themes deal with the most important concerns and with the fundamentals of the human condition. Like many writers, he has been called a regionalist. This is not quite fair, it is a limiting term. He represents this country, the Deep South, better than anyone else has ever done—with authenticity, with vividness, with a complete sense of conviction—but at the same time his work carries universal meanings.

Carvel Collins. Great writers are always compulsive writers, but then you have to have luck because the madhouses are full of compulsive writers who don't have any leverage and can't make it work. But Faulkner had a combination of compulsion and control which is phenomenal, and he had something to say, he addressed himself to significant problems. Someone asked Wiener, the mathematician, "How can you tell when a young person is going to be a good mathematician?" And Weiner said, "By the problems he chooses to work on." And I think Faulkner chose to work on things that are central to us all, and therefore the reader will be interested.

Narrator.   He had money now and fame. In 1952 he was the subject of a short film for television's series, "The Writer in America."

Phil Mullen.   One of the opening scenes was when I went out to his house and he met me at the door:

Faulkner: So, you're the one the trouble begins with.
Mullen: So, who did you want it to begin with?
Faulkner: Come in. Look, Phil, I don't see what my private life, the inside of my house, my family have got to do with my writing and the Nobel Foundation in Sweden.
Mullen: Bill, I'm not going to argue with you about anything, but all over this world people are reading what you're writing.

*I don't know whether you're all that good or not, but you've
got the Nobel Prize and people who read Faulkner would
like to know something about William Faulkner. Now, somebody's going to do the story and I'd like to do it.*
Faulkner: All right, do your story but no pictures.
*Mullen: Well, you let the high school paper make your pic-
ture, by golly.*
*Faulkner: Yes, but my daughter was editor of that paper, by
golly.*

Narrator.   For years Faulkner had fought for two things:
recognition and privacy. Now he had the recognition, but
no privacy at all.

He did not want to do the film, but when he was finally
persuaded, he cooperated with grace and good humor and
even contributed suggestions. He was filmed with old
friends such as Phil Stone and Mac Reed and with hunting
cronies and fellow townsmen.

Stone: You and the king have a good time?
*Faulkner: He's a fine gentleman, Stone. He even got along with
B. J., and you, if anybody, know how easy that is.*
Stone: That's true. Well, I was proud you finally made it.
Faulkner: Make that we did.
*Stone: Bill and I are getting to be old men now, and perhaps
someone who knows should say it—someone who knows that
he is even greater as a man than he is as a writer.*

Faulkner: Mornin', boys.
*Hunting Crony: I helped a fellow move a calf yesterday and I
hurt my hip.. He gimme seventy-five cents for helping him
move the calf—I had to spend a dollar sixty-five cents for
medicine. I'm gonna get rich if I keep that up.*
Faulkner: You sure will at that rate.

Narrator.   He was awkward, stiff, but it was a chance
for the public to see him, not dressed in a suit he wanted

110

to stuff and make people pay to see, but in his own element, with old friends.

Faulkner: Hello, Mac.
Reed: Why, Bill Faulkner, I'm glad to see you.
Faulkner: By the way, whatever happened to all those books of mine you loaded yourself up with?
Reed: Oh, I'm happy to tell you all of them have been sold, Bill. I understand that they're bringing pretty good prices now as collectors' items.
Faulkner: Funny how things turn out.

Narrator. He recreated the speech he had given at his daughter's high school graduation.

What threatens us today is fear. Not the atom bomb, nor even fear of it because if the bomb fell on Oxford tonight, all it could do would be to kill us which is nothing, since in doing that it will have robbed itself of its only power over us. . . . Our danger is the forces in the world today which are trying to use man's fear to rob him of his individuality, his soul, trying to reduce him to an unthinking mass by fear and bribery. It is not men in the masks who can and will save Man. It is Man

111

himself. . . . Man, the individual, men and women . . . who will believe always not only in the right of man to be free of injustice and rapacity and deception, but the duty and responsibility of man to see that justice and truth and pity and compassion are done. . . . Never be afraid to raise your voice for honesty and truth and compassion, against injustice and lying and greed. . . . you will change the earth. In one generation all the Napoleons and Hitlers and Caesars and Mussolinis and Stalins and all other tyrants who want power and aggrandisement, and the simple politicians and time-servers who themselves are merely baffled or ignorant or afraid, who have used, or are using, or hope to use man's fear and greed for man's enslavement, will have vanished from the face of it.

Narrator.   In November, 1952, Faulkner suffered a series of convulsions, ending in a hospital in Memphis. That winter Faulkner began drinking, suffered another series of convulsions, and ended up in the West Hills Sanitarium. There a trained psychiatrist diagnosed Faulkner's ailment as severe depression, prescribed electroshock therapy, and in six separate sessions coursed electricity through his brain.

Narrator.   In 1954 Faulkner finally finished his book, *A*

Fable. He had lived with it so long that he outlined the novel on the wall of his study. It remains there today.

Even though *A Fable* was awarded the National Book Award and a Pulitzer Prize, the critics were generally unfavorable.

Michel Mohrt.   I asked him a question, "Did you have in mind Marshall Foch of the First World War in your novel *A Fable*?" He got mad, he looked at me and said, "No!

Never! No, I had nobody in mind!" I said to myself, "My friend, you had better be quiet."

I'm a failed poet. Maybe every novelist wants to write poetry first, finds he can't, and then tries the short story, which is the most demanding form after poetry. And, failing at that, only then does he take up novel writing. (Jean Stein interview)

Narrator.   Actress Ruth Ford had been urging him for years to write her a play, until finally he was persuaded to explore the further adventures of Temple Drake, in the sequel to *Sanctuary*, *Requiem for a Nun*.

Ruth Ford (reads from the play.)   But, yet, it was like the dormitory at school. . . . The smell of women, all busy, thinking not about men, but just man, only a little stronger, sitting on the temporarily idle beds discussing the exigencies of their trade. Not me, not Temple. Shut up in that room twenty-four hours a day with nothing to do but hold fashion shows in the fur coat and flash pants, with nothing to see but a two-foot mirror and a Negro maid. Hanging bone-dry and safe in the middle of sin and pleasure. Like being suspended twenty fathoms deep, in an ocean diving bell. Be-

cause he wanted her to be contented, you see. But Temple didn't want to be just contented. So she had to do what us sportin' girls call, fall in love.

Narrator. Albert Camus' translation of *Requiem for a Nun* had a long run in France, but the American version closed quickly in New York.

Marc Connelly.   But I don't think Bill had any great hunger to be a playwright. He was at home in what he did, and he was so much at home there that he made his residence a pretty magnificent structure.

Narrator.   He talked about being tired, about the tank being nearly empty, about breaking the pencil. But he con-

tinued to write as he brought the Snopes saga to an end. The final doings of Flem Snopes and his kind were explored in *The Town* and *The Mansion*, which concluded the trilogy begun in 1940 with *The Hamlet*.

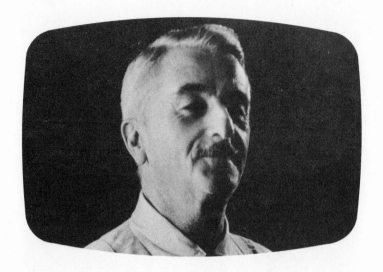

And finally Faulkner wrote his last book. One that was un-relieved comedy, that did not require interpretation, that did not tax the mind, that could be read easily, by any-one: *The Reivers*.

Phyllis Cerf Wagner.   When he finished this book, Bill came to New York and I said to him, "Ah, Bill, it's the funniest, the most wonderful book that I've ever read. It's my favorite." And he said, "I'm glad you like it, Miss Phyllis. When I read it," he said, "I just laugh and laugh."

Albert Erskine.   I had gone out to answer a phone call or something, and I came back, and he was sitting there looking at one page and laughing his head off.

Narrator.   In his last years he was, finally, financially se-cure. No more letters crying for help, for more time. Now he could, and did, turn down lucrative offers from Hol-lywood.

Jill Faulkner Summers.   I don't think he was being driven as much as he had been then. And I am sure that he wouldn't have been writing much longer. I think that he—well, he said so himself—he was written out.

Narrator.   In the late 50s, Faulkner had gone to the University of Virginia, as writer-in-residence, and to be near his daughter and grandchildren. He spent time in classes, gave lectures, and answered students' questions.

Faulkner: Respectability destroys one . . . . That is, nobody seems to be brave enough anymore to be an out-and-out blackguard or rascal, that sooner or later he's got to be respectable, and that finishes it.
Student: You said that you regard respectability as one of the prime enemies of individualism. Do you regard love as an enemy of individualism?
Faulkner: What's love got to do with respectability?

Narrator.   Having been an avid horseman all his life, he now took up a new and dangerous sport for a man of his years, fox hunting, riding to hounds. But it was elegant, British, dressy, an echo of his past.

Jill Faulkner Summers.　I think one reason he liked
fox hunting, not only for the dress-up part, was the element
of risk. It appealed to him. I think it appealed to him in
everything.

Narrator.   Hardly the best of riders, thrown with regularity, reckless, Faulkner broke ribs, collarbone, cracked his spine.

The horse, Stonewall, that Faulkner had ridden often, that had thrown him before, threw him again, hard. He took pills to ease the pain, but they didn't help. He began to drink, and that didn't help. A few days later he asked to be taken, as he had before, to the hospital in Byhalia, Mississippi.

The end of day is one vast green soundless murmur up the northwest toward the zenith. Yet it is as though light were not being subtracted from earth, drained from earth backward and upward into that cooling green, but rather had gathered, pooling for an unmoving moment yet, among the low places of the ground so that the ground, earth itself is luminous and only the dense clumps of trees are dark, standing darkly and immobile out of it.

And now, looking back and down, you see all Yoknapatawpha in the dying last of day beneath you. . . . yourself detached as God Himself for this moment above the cradle of your nativity

120

and of the men and women who made you, the record and chronicle of your native land proffered for your perusal in ring by concentric ring like the ripples on living water above the dreamless slumber of your past; you to preside unanguished and immune above this miniature of a man's passions and hopes and disasters—ambition and fear and lust and courage and ab- negation and pity and honor and sin and pride—all bound, pre- carious and ramshackle, held together by the web, the iron- thin warp and woof of his rapacity but withal yet dedicated to his dreams. (The Town)

Narrator. In the early hours of July 6, 1962, William Faulkner died. It was the Old Colonel's birthday.

*If there be grief, let it be the rain
And this but silver grief, for grieving's sake,
And these green woods be dreaming here to wake
Within my heart, if I should rouse again.*

*But I shall sleep, for where is any death
While in these blue hills slumbrous overhead
I'm rooted like a tree? Though I be dead
This soil that holds me fast will find me breath.*
("My Epitaph," in *A Green Bough*)

*And now I realise for the first time what an amazing gift I
had: uneducated in every formal sense, without even very literate,
let alone literary, companions, yet to have made the things I
made. I don't know where it came from.* (Letter to Joan Williams, April 19, 1953)

*It is my ambition to be . . . abolished and voided from history,
leaving it markless. . . . It is my aim, and every effort bent, that
the sum and history of my life, which in the same sentence
is my obit and epitaph too . . . "He made the books and he died."*
(Letter to Malcolm Cowley, February 11, 1949)

Robert Penn Warren.   I don't know why a person *should*
read anything, including the Holy Bible. I mean maybe we're
doomed to a world where nobody will read anything. Maybe we're doomed to be animals and go back to the caves.
I think a person who wants to be human should read
Faulkner. Now, if you're satisfied with your degree of hu-
manity and your understanding of human nature, don't read
him. But if you have any discontent or any aspiration to
be more human than you are, read him.

Partial funding for the film "**William Faulkner: A Life on
Paper**" was provided by a grant from the National
Endowment for the Humanities.

Credits

PRODUCER: Walt Lowe
DIRECTOR: Robert Squier
NARRATOR: Raymond Burr
VOICE OF FAULKNER: Arthur Ed Forman
ASSOCIATE PRODUCER: A. J. Jaeger
EDITOR: Sandra W. Bradley
COMPOSER: Ray Haney
CONCEIVED BY: George H. Wolfe
ADVISORS:
  Joseph Blotner
  Cleanth Brooks
  Panthea Broughton
  Carvel Collins
  Curtis Davis
  Shelby Foote
  Evans Harrington
  Louis D. Rubin Jr.
  Lewis P. Simpson
  Ben Wasson
PRINCIPAL PHOTOGRAPHY: Larry Couzens
ADDITIONAL PHOTOGRAPHY:
  Joe Akin
  Rob Cooper
  Gilbert Dassonville
  Ludwig Goon
  A. J. Jaeger
  George Johnson
  Walt Lowe
  J. Chris McGuire
  Ben Tubb
  Robert Squier
CAMERA ASSISTANTS:
  Ed Grey
  Philip Holahan
  Jeff Kimbal
  Joel Markowitz
  Phil Swetz
GRIPS: Mike Wilson
       Nino Celano
AUDIO RECORDINGS:
  Rob Cooper
  Chris McGuire
  Ron Yoshida

AUDIO MIX: **Nelson Funk**
PRODUCTION ASSISTANT: **Stephanie Bobo**
LOCATION ASSISTANCE: **Judith Couzens**
Julie P. Davis
ACTORS:
Mona Britt
Steve Brown
Cheri Burney
Ken Davis
Gene Ericson
Steve Kelly
Jon Mallard
D. W. Miller
Dale McIntire
Larry Thomas
ACKNOWLEDGEMENTS:
William Boozer
Col. Cofield
Jack Cofield
Neal & Janis Gregory
Harold Ober Associates
Liveright Publishers
Louise Meadow
Ed Meek
Carl Peterson
MGM Studios
Random House Publishers
Ben Wasson
James Webb
Dean Faulkner Wells
Lawrence Wells

John Davis Williams Library
University of Mississippi

Alderman Library
University of Virginia

**SPECIAL THANKS IS GIVEN TO JILL FAULKNER
SUMMERS AND TO YOKNAPATAWPHA PRESS FOR
USE OF STILL PHOTOGRAPHS FROM THE BOOK
"WILLIAM FAULKNER, THE COFIELD COLLECTION"**

**AND TO THE CITIZENS AND THE CITY OF OXFORD
FOR THEIR GENEROUS ASSISTANCE IN THE
MAKING OF THIS FILM**

Photography Credits

Photographs of William Faulkner and his family were used through the courtesy of the following individuals: William Boozer, Carvel Collins, Ed Meek, Phil Mullins, Ben Wasson, and Dean Faulkner Wells. Reproductions of Faulkner's drawings along with scenes from the Ole Miss campus were supplied by the University of Mississippi Library, Department of Archives and Special Collections. Grateful appreciation for the use of these photographs is extended by the Mississippi Authority for Educational Television and the University Press of Mississippi.

**Other books on Faulkner
from the University Press of Mississippi**

*The South and Faukner's Yoknapatawpha:
The Actual and the Apocryphal, 1976*
Edited by Evans Harrington and Ann J. Abadie. 224 pp. $8.95
(cloth); $3.95 (paper).

*The Maker and the Myth:
Faulkner and Yoknapatawpha, 1977*
Edited by Evans Harrington and Ann J. Abadie. 183 pp. $8.95
(cloth); $3.95 (paper).

*Faulkner, Modernism and Film:
Faulkner and Yoknatapawpha, 1978*
Edited by Evans Harrington and Ann J. Abadie. 214 pp. $12.50
(cloth); $6.95 (paper).

*Fifty Years of Yoknapatawpha:
Faulkner and Yoknapatawpha, 1979*
Edited by Doreen Fowler and Ann J. Abadie. 300 pp. $15.95
(cloth); $7.95 (paper).

The above four volumes make available the proceedings
of the past four Faulkner and Yoknapatawpha Conferences
sponsored annually by the University of Mississippi.

A Faulkner Miscellany
Edited by James B. Meriwether. 176 pp. $2.00 (cloth).

William Faulkner's "The Wild Palms": A Study
By Thomas L. McHaney. 230 pp. $3.00 (cloth).

*Old Tales and Talking: Quentin Compson in William
Faulkner's "Absalom, Absalom!" and Related Works*
By Estella Schoenberg. 167 pp. $7.95 (cloth).